love letters (unfinished)

love letters (unfinished)

a collection of love poems, told in real time

by lorelei j.p. bowman

Copyright © 2025 Laurel Whitman

All rights reserved.

To get in touch with the author, email hello@curiocontent.co

Paperback ISBN: 978-1-0681523-0-6
E-book ISBN: 978-1-0681523-1-3

for my wife, Jemma

happy first wedding anniversary

thank you for being my lighthouse

contents

before

    love letters   11

2018

    suddenly   15

2019

    pillow talk   19
    j.r.   21
    she   22
    a poem for her   25
    leave the door unlocked   27

2020

    heaven/hell   31
    how did the sky look?   33
    dawn   35
    pink   37
    (un)earthly pleasures   38
    blinds   41

2021

    intertwined   45
    anomaly   46
    safe & sound   49
    shoreditch   51

2022

	shield	54
	polaris	56
	foundations	58

2023

	i touched the universe and it hugged me back	62
	gratitude	67

2024

	treasure / fragments	71
	bloom	73
	prologue	75

before

love letters (unfinished)

love letters

cover me in all the love letters
i have ever written
and set me on fire

love letters (unfinished)

love letters (unfinished)

2018

love letters (unfinished)

suddenly

isn't it strange
how most feelings come
either all at once or not at all.

but you are not like that
you are like a slow winter sunrise on the horizon
or the warm glow of sunlight slipping through my window
you are like the ocean tide lapping at the shore
pulling me into you one grain of sand at a time
you are like sleepy sunday mornings with no alarm set
or the way streetlights flicker on one by one away up a hill
you were both sudden and slow
you are a tempo i never knew existed

love letters (unfinished)

2019

love letters (unfinished)

pillow talk

i've never been someone who could sleep next to other people.
i like my own space
slow breathing and loud dreaming
lights off, fan on
i like the dent in my pillows

so when you fall asleep, and i can feel your little twitches of slumber
and feel your body falling against mine
i slowly ease my arms out from around you, millimetre by millimetre
my arms are tense from my body trying not to breathe so loudly
and my hands are starting to go numb from trying to stay still

so i quietly pull away putting my hand on your ribs, your chest, your arm, your back
leaving a trail of my fingerprints on your skin where you can still feel me
a silent nightly ritual so as not to wake you
because i cannot get to sleep when i'm holding someone
but i cannot bear to not hold you.

i've never been someone who could sleep next to other people.
and even though i cannot get to sleep when i'm holding you
i would take all the numb arms and aching necks
because it is worth it just to feel you fall asleep inside my arms
i would take all the pausing movements and bated breaths

than to ever sleep without you again

love letters (unfinished)

love letters (unfinished)

j.r.

i can think of nothing better
than coming home to you every day
for the rest of my life

love letters (unfinished)

she

she feels like vines climbing up a fence to spread big green leaves and tiny yellow flowers
she feels like a new pair of socks and fresh sheets from the dryer
she feels like saturday mornings with no alarm set
she feels like shells on a beach and smooth seaglass that the tide has brought in
she feels like gentle kisses on soft scarred skin and never letting go
she feels like sweet black coffee and cinnamon buns on a sunny morning
she feels like the first star in the sky at night and the first glimpse of sun on the horizon
she feels like sunrays creeping through my window and falling on cold morning skin
she feels like tea stains in cups and empty toothpaste tubes
she feels like dust sparkling in a beam of sunlight and rainbows refracting on my carpet
she feels like sunflowers growing from the soil up to the sky and turning to face the sun
she feels like naked legs tangled up in bedsheets
she feels like fresh washed hair and the smell of fresh cut grass
she feels like the shift of sunlight breaking between bright green leaves
she feels like uncontrollable laughter until your stomach hurts
she feels like the rest of my life all in one breath
she makes loving her feel as natural as breathing
she makes me want to love myself, too
she makes the sunshine okay
she makes me feel like i am filled with light and it is pouring out

of the cracks in my skin
she makes me feel like everything will be alright

love letters (unfinished)

a poem for her

how sweet it is
to love someone
the way that i love you
like wildflowers
growing from a hedgerow
or a city kid
seeing the ocean for the first time
how sweet it is
to get to love you
to make you tea on sunday mornings
and hear you call me baby
how sweet it is
to be loved by you
and to get to call you mine

love letters (unfinished)

leave the door unlocked

when she's away
it's like the edges of reality start to fray,
like the side of her bed neatly made up
no empty mug by the bathroom mirror
from her morning tea

i lock the door behind me when i get home.

i stay on my side of the sofa.
it's just for a night, a day or two
but existing in this space without her
feels like walking down a street in your hometown
when all the buildings have changed

i make her bedtime tea anyway.

soon she'll be home
her singing in the bathroom
the smell of mac & cheese down the hallway
her shoes by the door
i'll leave the door open when i get home tomorrow

i hope to god i never have to leave the door locked.

love letters (unfinished)

love letters (unfinished)

2020

love letters (unfinished)

heaven/hell

how strange
that before i knew you
heaven looked so very different
and i didn't even realise i was wrong

how odd
that once i knew you
the only hell worth fearing
was one where you weren't here

love letters (unfinished)

how did the sky look?

the sky was navy on the day we met
you got lost on the way
and i saw you come in
cold from the november chill
all long legs and red lips
i remember
the crystal pendant over your top
and the soy latte you ordered
but wouldn't let me pay for

the sky was heavy
rain falling in torrents
after we stepped out
when the cafe finally closed
huddled under a canopy
of two umbrellas
both longing for the other
to be the bolder one
neither was

the sky was alive
with stars and raindrops intermingling
as i walked home after
i closed my umbrella
and let the rain fall on me
i felt fresh
clean, for the first time in so long
that night
the sky was ours

love letters (unfinished)

love letters (unfinished)

dawn

like dawn cresting the horizon
casting an unbent and unbroken light
your love spread through me
and reached its golden fingers, unwavering
straight into my soul

love letters (unfinished)

pink

pink, is the colour of her lipstick in springtime
pink, is the colour of her softest pyjamas
pink, is the colour of the card she gave me for our first valentine's
pink, is the colour of her sofa which we pushed all the way to her flat
pink, is the colour of the jumper she wore when she first met my parents
pink, is the colour of the foxgloves in our secret spot
pink, is the colour of her eyeshadow on our first date
the truth is, you could give me any colour
and i could name a hundred things that remind me of her
being with her is like experiencing the world in technicolour
after you thought your eyes were only capable of seeing
black and white

love letters (unfinished)

(un)earthly pleasures

i do not believe in a higher power
i don't hold faith that someone
out there will answer my prayers.

but i do believe there is more than us,
worlds and galaxies floating
lightyears away, hanging in the air

so if earthly pleasures are
those which are of this earth
then my love for you is not one

the hum of your lips on my skin
like white noise when you first wake up
the taste of your name in my mouth

like a glimpse of outerspace
these things are not of this earth
my love for you, is not earthly

the love beating inside me
pumping through my veins
filling up my brain in a cloud

your love is *otherworldly*

so if earthly pleasures
are those which are of this earth
and if a hand should strike us down for those

i will go on loving you
for my love is unearthly; heavenly

and it will last far longer than just this life

love letters (unfinished)

love letters (unfinished)

blinds

the way the morning light
falls onto her face
as she pulls up the blinds
is a kind of happiness
i never knew i was missing
until the thought of being without it

love letters (unfinished)

2021

love letters (unfinished)

intertwined

candyfloss clouds at dusk
swirls of dusty pink
and wisps of lilac
entangled with forget-me-not blue

the shift of a faint breeze
on the hottest summer's day
in the lapping waves
of airless august

soft petals curling open
to greet the morning dew
cautious fingertips fluttering
over downy leaves

i see you everywhere
in each speck of sunlit dust
and every grain of sand
in the way nature glows around you

you are of the earth
and one with her
rooted in the world
just as you are rooted in my soul

intertwined
two beings come together
with roots that neither belong to me
nor you anymore; only us

love letters (unfinished)

anomaly

i never thought someone would stay this long
but here you are
nine hundred and seventy four days later
and you're still here
like a shadow watching over me
and a reflection of all the good things i could be
i don't know how you do it
putting up with my rainy days
and all the work i have left to do
all i know is that you are the one thing i cannot explain

i do not believe the universe has some great plan
i think we are all simply floating through time and space,
collections of particles experiencing moments
in our own unplanned timelines
but you? you are an anomaly
you make me question everything i thought i believed
so unwaveringly

for you are the one thing i cannot chalk up to a series of decisions
or a random coincidence in my life's timeline
you are the one thing i cannot be cynical about

because i feel you in the soles of my feet when i'm walking
and the palm of my hands holding my morning coffee
i see you in the way a raindrop rolls down a window pane
or a child chases falling leaves
the way the moon looks at 2am

and the sound of you sleeping next to me
when i'm wide awake
i feel you in my lungs when i breathe

you make me want to be better
you make me believe i could be

so i do not believe in fate,
or everything happening for a reason
i think we are all only travelling along our own timelines
fumbling through life in a series of decisions and random coincidences
but when it comes to you,
you are inexplicable
because how could something as extraordinarily wonderful
as being loved by you
possibly be by chance?

love letters (unfinished)

love letters (unfinished)

safe & sound

she is soft in the way she kisses me
she is gentle in the way she speaks to me
she is tender in the way she holds me
but oh how she is fierce in the way she loves me
with no holding back and no false pretences
fiercely is the way you love the world
with hope in your heart
even when it feels heavy
fiercely is the way you protect
those around you, even when we don't deserve it

i have never seen a flower as beautiful as she is strong
as gentle as she is fierce
as brave as she is nervous
but you defy all understanding, my love

for you are the not the thorny rose, though you are as beautiful as one
no, you are the climbing ivy
which will not be moved for the strongest storm, even if it shakes
you are the oak tree who has been standing tall
for longer we can imagine
and will be here long after we are gone

you are the fields of purple heather
that stand battered atop blustery mountains
and the stems of foxgloves which are as sweet as they are deadly
you are kindness, and sweetness, and all things good incarnate
for you love me gently, but oh so fiercely, too

love letters (unfinished)

love letters (unfinished)

shoreditch

neon lights
overpriced cocktails
dancing at the table
rainy nights
in noisy cities
and the way you make
anywhere
feel like where i'm meant to be

love letters (unfinished)

2022

shield

there are some things i wish that may never come to pass
i wish for time,
i wish for a quiet mind
i wish for my life to be so void of grief i forget its name

i wish that i could tell you i have slain all the demons
and you are free to dance in the sunshine freely
i wish i could give you my eyes to see yourself clearly
and my voice to speak to yourself with all the love
that burns inside me
but i do not have such power

i have nothing to give but myself
so i give you this, my heart—and my word

i offer you a promise:

i promise that i will try to keep you safe
and if i cannot keep you safe
i promise i will keep you loved
i will tend to your wounds
and when i cannot mend them
i will stay and hold you until they are healed

i wish i could tell you i have fixed everything
that i have ventured on and stopped the war
but i am only me
and sometimes my best will not be good enough
and sometimes my love will not be enough
to quiet the voices in your head

and calm the sadness in your heart
but even when it is not enough
my best, and my love, are yours

i will stand with you in your fight
my hand, and my heart i pledge to you
in this life
and beyond the timelines and universes we see
you have my heart
i will stand beside you always
and i will be your shield, if you let me

for i can offer nothing but myself

love letters (unfinished)

polaris

she holds me for hours
opens a window
to bring the night in
to show me the stars
she says
remember how small we are
specks of dust
floating on a rock in space

she turns the lights down
because they hurt my eyes
she puts the fan on and holds me
so i cannot remember what it feels like
to be lonely
i empty my mind into the void
and soak tears through her shirt
she brings me dry pyjamas

she holds me
and even when it all feels too much
like i am a hurricane
she makes me feel safe
when i am a maelstrom, she is the lighthouse
my anchor
the sea and the stars all at once
navigating me home

she wraps me in the blanket
and puts water on my wrists

i am shivering
she holds me,
and kisses my face
i am safe
i am loved
she is the north star in my bedroom

love letters (unfinished)

foundations

when you are concrete,
i will hold you
as you are laying foundations,
that will last for years to come
i will hold you
and when you are an oak tree,
weathering any storm mother nature can throw at you
i will stand steady beside you

when you are delicate like gossamer
glistening with morning dew,
threads tangled and thin as lightbeams
i will hold you,
and i will love you
when you are torn paper
fraying edges and muddled words
spilled ink and tear-streaked pages
i will love you

i will hold you
when you are the tallest skyscraper
and when you are the smallest speck of stardust
when you are stormy and cannot sail
for the waves are too fierce
when they crash on the bow and flood the deck
i will be your lifeboat
when the lighthouse is hidden by cloud
and you are drenched in darkness

i will be your moon,
and i will guide you home

when you are resilient,
and when you are tired
when you are mighty,
and when you feel you can't go on
whether you are scattered flower petals
or leaves in the gutter
i will hold you
and i will love you,
always.

love letters (unfinished)

love letters (unfinished)

2023

i touched the universe and it hugged me back

my love
if i could walk the earth with my hands out
and catch all the raindrops, so you only ever had sunny days,
i would

if i could fly to space
and pluck the stars out of the sky
so i could hang them outside your window,
i would rearrange them to spell 'you are beautiful'

if i could give you every breath from my lungs
and every beat from my heart,
i would
because they are already yours and i do not need them

for i breathe you in with every mouthful of air
and every beat of the earth
and i need nothing else

if i could explain to you
that when i touch you it makes me question
whether maybe there is a heaven and i have already been there
if i could make you understand
that when i kiss you it is the only time
my thoughts are ever truly quiet

but i cannot explain this
because there is no way to make you truly understand

what it is like to be in love with the moon and watch her rise for
you each day
because how could you know what it is like to touch the sun
and be unburned
how could you know what it is like to bathe in pure light
whenever i am around you
what it is like to be in love with the blues of the ocean
or the haze of twilight

it is indescribable but i will try

if i could i would fight every person on this earth
just to give you one night of peaceful sleep
i would charge into battle
armed with nothing but my love for you and a soul on fire,
just to give you restful dreams

if i could, i would take every bad thing in this world
and every bad thing that is ever to happen,
and i would tie them all up
and bury them deep inside myself so they could never reach you

i would grow a thorny coat and wrap myself around you,
i would fly you to a distant planet filled with fresh spring
blossoms
and pots of perfectly brewed tea and fluffy jumpers

i would bleed myself dry just to give you a second of knowing
how utterly perfect you are
but you will never know
because how can you know what it is
to have the taste of pure sunshine when we kiss

love letters (unfinished)

or watch a flower grow before you and know it blooms just for you

how can you know what it's like to see every possibility
for how your life could go,
but instead of feeling scared–
feel comforted, and safe and content,
knowing that no matter which one comes,
you will be there and so nothing truly bad can happen

how can you know what it is like to touch outerspace
and feel the pulse of the universe in your fingertips,
and know that every ounce of blackness
and every drop of starlight, is made for you

you can never know that
so you can never truly know how it feels to love you,
and be loved by you
but i can, and i will forever know
that i touched the universe,
and she smiled at me
and it was your smile in those stars

love letters (unfinished)

love letters (unfinished)

love letters (unfinished)

gratitude

thank you for being the voice when i have no words
for being my tether when i feel i'm going to float away
thank you for being the life boat when i am drowning myself
the open arms when i feel unloveable

thank you for being the steady hand when i feel i'm about to fall
the soft touch which brings me back when i am numb
and the cool night breeze when i feel on fire
thank you for being the only thing that makes my brain quiet

thank you for carrying me when i cannot climb anymore
and thank you for being my lungs when i cannot breathe anymore
for being my anchor, my compass
and my lighthouse all at the same time

i know i am heavy to hold
but you make me feel like one day i may be light
i know i am too much and not enough all at once
but you make me feel like one day i may be just enough

thank you for making the stars feel so close
and the darkness seem so far away
thank you for keeping me grounded
thank you for staying

love letters (unfinished)

2024

love letters (unfinished)

treasure / fragments

i bring you the worst parts of me
like fragments of your favourite mug
a handful of seashells collected from the shoreline
that go dull when they dry
i display them like a magpie
waiting for it
you only take the shattered pieces
and hold them together
where i see holes, you say
just look how the light shines in

love letters (unfinished)

bloom

she is like a sunflower
and i will happily bask
in her golden glow
for the rest of my days
building myself
as a fence around her
to protect from those
who would cast shadow
and wither her leaves

love letters (unfinished)

prologue

crisp leaves and clear skies
wisps of cloud
you in white
the smell of almost-autumn
holding my breath

as they count me down
i feel nothing
except every part of me is fizzing
five, four, three, two, one
i turn

and you are there
like always
and like never before
can i kiss her?
time tumbles past us

swept up in the joy of it all
trying to savour each moment
like grains of sand
through my fingers
too many to possibly hold

nothing is real but you
the ink still wet
on the page of our next chapter
your eyes and mine
the beginning of forever

love letters (unfinished)

~~the end~~

the beginning

about the author

Lorelei J. P. Bowman (Whitman) is a writer and word-lover from the South Coast of England, UK. From prose and poetry to copywriting and content marketing, Lorelei's never met a kind of writing they don't like. After accumulating almost two decades' worth of poems, they decided it was time to put (digital) pen to (physical) paper and self-publish their first collection of poems. Serendipitously, the timing coincided with Lorelei deciding what to gift their wife, Jemma, for the couple's first wedding anniversary. All-too-fitting for a paper anniversary, it seemed only right to create a physical book comprising of all the secret love letters Lorelei's written for Jemma over the years.

www.ingramcontent.com/pod-product-compliance
Lightning Source LLC
Chambersburg PA
CBHW040246010526
44119CB00057B/836